ANIMAL

RIGHTS

CHARLES PATTERSON

ENSLOW PUBLISHERS, INC.

Bloy St. & Ramsey Ave.   P.O. Box 38
Box 777   Aldershot
Hillside, N.J. 07205   Hants GU12 6BP
U.S.A.   U.K.

For

Minima, Maxima, and Marilyn

Library of Congress Cataloging-in-Publication Data

Patterson, Charles.
    Animal rights/Charles Patterson.
      p. cm
    Includes index.
    Summary: Discusses the ways in which animals are used for medical
research, food, education, and entertainment, and presents the views
of some people concerned with the treatment of animals.
    ISBN 0-89490-468-X
    1. Animal rights—Juvenile literature. [1. Animal rights,
2. Animals—Treatment.] I. Title.
HV4708.P38 1993
179'.3—dc20   92-44286
                                                 CIP
                                                 AC

Printed in the United States of America

10 9 8 7 6 5 4 3 2 1

Illustration Credits: American Anti-Vivisection Society, p. 47; American
Association for the Prevention of Cruelty to Animals (ASPCA), pp. 9,
19; Jody Boyman/Progressive Animal Welfare Society (PAWS), p. 22;
Dan Brinzac, p. 12; Mary Byrne, p. 93; Farm Sanctuary, p. 68; Food
and Drug Administration, p. 50; The Fund for Animals, Inc., p. 76;
Pat Graham, p. 29; Humane Farming Association, pp. 63, 65; Marilyn
J. Klein, p. 16, 80; National Anti-Vivisection Society, pp. 32; Noah's
Ark Rehabilitation Center, p. 91; People for the Ethical Treatment of
Animals (PETA), pp. 35, 45, 54, 82, 87.

Cover Photo: People for the Ethical Treatment of Animals (PETA)

CONTENTS

1 A GROWING CONCERN   5

2 ANIMALS AS COMPANIONS   15

3 ANIMALS IN EDUCATION.   27

4 ANIMAL RESEARCH   41

5 THE ANIMALS WE EAT   59

6 HUNTING, TRAPPING,
AND ENTERTAINMENT   73

7 RESCUE AND REFUGE.   89

NOTES BY CHAPTER.   101

FURTHER READING   108

INDEX   111

1
A GROWING CONCERN

Georgi Rosen is opposed to fur coats. She doesn't drink Coca-Cola either. Coke sponsors rodeos, she says, and rodeos are mean to animals. Georgi, who is 11 and is in the sixth grade, does all she can to help animals. She even writes letters of protest to companies that use animals to test their products.

When she is in a restaurant, Georgi asks about each dish's ingredients so she can avoid meat. She became a vegetarian two years ago at the age of nine. Georgi's interest in animals is on display in her room at home where she is surrounded by 61 stuffed animals, 4 caged birds, 3 dogs, and a guinea pig.

Georgi is against dissection too. She has not yet been asked to dissect a frog in school, but she knows she could never do it. "They're getting killed, and killing is harming," she explains. A poster printed by People for the Ethical Treatment of Animals (PETA) hangs on her bedroom wall. PETA is a large animal rights group that counts Georgi as a member. The poster shows a frog. The message under it reads, "Don't cut me up. Cut out dissection."

Georgi lives in East Providence, Rhode Island. Recently a newspaper wrote about her campaign against dissection. Georgi doesn't think it's fair to force students to dissect animals if they don't want to. She lobbied Senator Myrth York, a woman who represents Georgi's neighborhood in the state legislature, with phone calls and letters. Georgi also circulated a petition that collected 200 signatures. As a result, Senator York introduced in the state legislature a bill that would require teachers to provide their students with the option of doing a non-animal assignment in place of dissection. The bill was sent to the Senate Health, Education, and Welfare Committee.

"I was impressed, this is one smart kid," said Senator York. "Plus, the issue touched a nerve in me because I remember not taking biology in high school because I didn't want to dissect frogs."

A zoology professor at the University of Rhode Island spoke out against the bill. When he said alternatives to dissection are not as good as a real frog, Georgi disagreed. "There are many alternatives to dissection, such as Ribbits, which are cloth model frogs," she wrote in a letter to Senator York. "Ribbits also are very helpful because they don't have to be thrown away; so in the end, Ribbits will cost less too."

Georgi's mother, who is not a vegetarian, respects her daughter's commitment. "She believes so strongly in something," she says proudly, "and then she really tries to do something constructive about it. I think that channeling your energy to something you really believe in is important."[1]

The bill passed the Senate but died in committee in the House during the 1992 state legislative session. However, the lawmakers passed a resolution urging teachers to find non-animal alternatives to classroom dissection. Georgi and Senator York plan on reintroducing the bill when the legislature reconvenes.

Background

For centuries human beings have used animals for food, clothing, and work. As people grew in number, cleared land for crops, and built roads, towns, and cities, wild animals were driven from their habitats. Humans hunted animals for food, killed them for fur, experimented on them, and used them for transportation, sport, and entertainment. For most of history, humans thought animals existed only to serve them. People who struggled to survive against famine, disease, and death gave little thought to animal welfare.

The Bible says that God gave man "dominion over the fish of the sea, and over the fowl of the air, and over every living thing that moveth upon the earth" (Genesis 1:28). The Greek philosopher Aristotle declared that nature made animals "for the sake of man."[2]

René Descartes (1596-1650)—who is called the father of modern philosophy—said humans and animals are completely different. Human beings possess consciousness and immortal souls while animals have neither souls nor consciousness. Descartes said animals are like machines. They are incapable of feeling pain. They only *seem* to suffer. Descartes and his colleagues used to cut open live dogs to see how they "worked."

In the eighteenth century the first signs of a different point of view appeared. In 1776 an English clergyman published the first book ever to recommend treating animals with kindness. The English philosopher Jeremy Bentham (1748–1832) looked forward to the day "when the rest of the animal creation may acquire those rights which never could have been withholden from them but by the hand of tyranny."[3]

In 1822 England passed the world's first law against cruelty to certain animals. Two years later the first animal welfare organization—the Society for the Prevention of Cruelty to Animals—was founded in London.

In the United States the first animal welfare group— the American Society for the Prevention of Cruelty to Animals (ASPCA)—began in 1866. Its founder was Henry Bergh, President Lincoln's ambassador to Russia during the Civil War. One day while walking in the Russian capital

Henry Bergh founded the American Society for the Prevention of Cruelty to Animals in 1866. The ASPCA is the oldest animal protection organization in the United States.

of St. Petersburg, Bergh saw a horse struggling to pull a heavy cart up a hill until it collapsed under the load and fell to its knees. Instead of showing pity, the driver beat the horse unmercifully. Bergh intervened, but the experience left him shaken. He realized how defenseless animals were and how they needed people to speak up for them.

When Bergh got back to New York, he raised enough money to start the ASPCA. He also persuaded the state legislature of New York to pass a law that made cruelty to animals a criminal offense. It was the first such law in America.

Other animal welfare groups were formed. Anti-vivisection societies that opposed experiments on dogs and other animals (called *vivisection*) also sprang up. However, growing anti-vivisectionist opposition to the animal research did not stop the experiments. Medical advances were convincing the public that research on animals was important for medical progress.[4]

The Birth of a Movement

In 1975 Peter Singer's book, *Animal Liberation,* was published. Singer was an Australian philosopher who questioned the assumption that we humans have the right to do anything we want to animals simply because they are not human. He argued that since non-human animals are sentient beings who feel pain and pleasure, we need to respect their interests. Their lives are as important to them, he said, as our lives are to us.

Singer called the failure to give the interests of animals "equal consideration" *speciesism*. Singer defined speciesism as the prejudice of our species against other species and compared it to *racism* and *sexism*. Racism is the belief by one race that it is superior to other races, while sexism is the belief that one sex is better than the other. Just as the enslavement of African Americans and the oppression of women were once acceptable, before they were later discredited, so Singer believes the enslavement and oppression of animals is a wrong that society needs to correct.

In 1976, the year after the publication of Singer's book, the first large public demonstrations on behalf of animals took place in front of the American Museum of Natural History in New York City. Cat lovers discovered that in the museum basement two experimental psychologists were conducting experiments on cats to study the neurological bases of sexual behavior. The experiments, which were funded by the National Institutes of Health (NIH), involved cutting out parts of the cats' brains, severing their nerves, and destroying their sense of smell. The protesters denounced the experiments as cruel, expensive, and unnecessary.

Museum officials refused to discuss the issue with the demonstrators. The protests continued week after week until the Museum received so much unfavorable publicity

The first large public demonstrations on behalf of animals took place in 1976 at the Museum of Natural History in New York City. The demonstrators were protesting experiments on cats that involved cutting out parts of their brains.

and so much criticism from its members that it eventually stopped the research and closed the lab.

Since the late 1970s hundreds of thousands of Americans have become active in the growing animal rights movement. Animal rights activists have gained the attention of the media and the public with their protests against research laboratories, cosmetic companies, fur ranches, stockyards, and other businesses and institutions that use animals. Membership in the older and more established animal welfare organizations and anti-vivisection societies also increased. It is estimated that today there are as many as 7,000 animal protection organizations in the United States with a combined membership of 10 million people. Congress says that it receives more calls and letters about animal welfare than about any other issue.

Interest seems especially high among young people. Many schools have animal rights groups and after school clubs. In 1991 a Gallup Youth Survey found that two out of three teenagers in America support animal rights (41% said they supported the goals of the animal rights movement "very much" while 26% said they supported it "somewhat").

However, using animals for food, clothing, experiments, and entertainment has a long history. The animal rights movement, which is still very young, is meeting resistance from those who support the use of animals for human benefit, especially researchers, furriers, hunters, farmers, and others who feel most threatened by the movement's success. While most people oppose cruelty to animals, many disapprove of those who spray red paint on fur coats or break into laboratories to free animals and damage equipment. If it comes down to a choice between people and animals, they say, human rights are more important than animal rights.

2
ANIMALS
AS COMPANIONS

In the United States there are over 55 million cats and 45 million dogs. Unfortunately, many of them have been abandoned. They are kittens and puppies left by the roadside or inside dumpsters. They are strays who must fend for themselves in alleys and abandoned buildings. Every year millions of these homeless animals die from disease and starvation. Many are killed by cars and trucks. Those who survive do so without adequate care or nourishment. There are simply too many cats and dogs and not enough homes to take care of them.

The great tragedy is that each year millions of cats and dogs who end up in pounds and shelters have to be destroyed. Pounds and shelters are forced to kill four out of five of the cats and dogs they receive because nobody will adopt them. They may be injured or too old, or maybe

These two cats—a mother (foreground) and her daughter—were strays before the author adopted them and had them spayed. They now live in an apartment in New York City.

they are just not cute or friendly enough. The problem is made worse when people insist on buying their new pet from a breeder or pet store rather than adopt one of the doomed homeless strays at a shelter.

The Overpopulation Problem

Cats and dogs reproduce much more rapidly than humans do, thanks to early puberty, short pregnancies and large litters. Dogs reproduce about 15 times faster than humans, cats about 45 times faster. Over a six-year period one female dog and her offspring can be the source of 67,000 puppies. In just seven years one female cat and her young can produce 420,000 cats.

While nature is partly to blame, human beings bear much of the responsibility for the overpopulation problem. Too many people, out of ignorance or irresponsibility, let their pets reproduce. It begins when they let their unneutered male or unspayed female roam around the neighborhood. Or they might decide to mate their pet with that of a friend or neighbor to let their children see "the miracle of birth."

Homes cannot always be found for these new kittens or puppies. People end up either abandoning them or giving them away to somebody else who may abandon them later. Some people keep the offspring and let them reproduce when they grow up, thus adding further to the overpopulation problem. Or people may turn them in to their local shelter. "Some days there's a constant stream of people coming in with their laundry baskets full of kittens," reported the manager of one city shelter. If the animals are not adopted quickly, the shelter is forced to kill them to make room for new arrivals.

The people who want purebred pets are willing to spend lots of money to get them. They might use them to breed more pets. But when these cats or dogs are bred and sold, there are that many more dogs and cats in shelters who will have to be killed because there is nobody to adopt them.

Spaying and Neutering

Altering cats and dogs so that they can no longer reproduce is the best solution to the pet overpopulation problem. Female pets are spayed and male pets are neutered. When these surgical procedures are performed by licensed veterinarians, they are perfectly safe and painless. Female pets should be spayed at six to nine months of age, shortly after their first heat. Male pets should be neutered soon after they reach maturity which is about the same age. Spaying and neutering will prevent the litters that too often bring neglect, starvation, injury, and finally death to unwanted animals.

Some people think pets will be better off left alone, but this is not true. Early spaying of female pets reduces the risk of uterine diseases and other health risks associated

These are cats at the ASPCA shelter in New York City. Four out of five animals in shelters have to be put to death because there are not enough homes for them.

with pregnancy and birth. Early neutering of males eliminates the likelihood of testicular tumors and prostrate problems. Also, altered animals feel less frustration. They are less prone to get into fights or run out in front of cars. Most important of all, altering one's pet helps control the pet population explosion. Owners who do not alter their pets are the biggest reason for the tragedy of pet overpopulation.

Euthanasia

Shelters, pounds, and humane societies do society's "dirty work" by killing between 10 and 13 million cats and dogs each year. When shelters receive abandoned, abused, and homeless strays, they have the thankless job of killing four out of five of them.

Pounds and shelters put their unwanted cats and dogs to death by means of *euthanasia* ("kind death"). The most humane way to euthanize an animal is by injection. When sodium pentobarbital is injected into an animal's vein, it brings a quick and relatively painless death. However, many pounds and shelters use less expensive and more painful methods. These include gassing, electrocution, and suffocation in a decompression chamber.

Part of the tragedy about the millions of animals who are put to death every year is that most of them are young, healthy animals. The majority of them are less than one year old. If an animal isn't adopted quickly, the shelter must euthanize him or her to make room for the new arrivals. Shelters will wait anywhere from a few days to a couple of weeks.

Some people criticize pounds and shelters for killing animals, but these places have little choice. They are certainly not responsible for the pet overpopulation problem. In fact, shelters and humane societies are in the forefront of the campaign to educate the public about the problem. Many shelters offer low-cost spay-and-neuter programs to the public.

The American Society for the Prevention of Cruelty to Animals (ASPCA) in New York takes in more unwanted animals than any other organization in the United States. It tries its best to find homes for them, but there are just not enough willing people. Like other shelters, the ASPCA must euthanize the animals nobody will adopt.

At its Manhattan shelter every day shortly after three o'clock, the director makes her rounds to decide which animals will be euthanized that day. In front of each cage she examines the animal, reviews the history, and marks her decision on the chart. An assistant has the job of bringing the condemned ones to the staff persons who will euthanize them with sodium pentobarbital. He tries to make the animals feel as comfortable as possible. "I play with them, pet them, and am often the last thing they see on earth," he says. "Many of these animals get more love in these last few seconds than they had in their whole lives." [1]

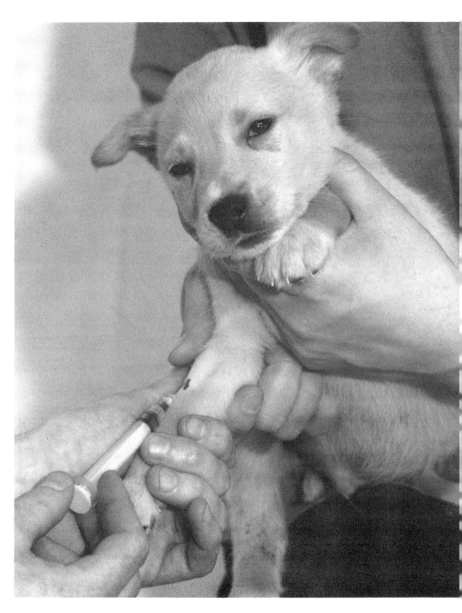

Workers at a shelter in Washington State give a lethal injection to a puppy named Buster. Millions of dogs and cats have to be put to death each year in the United States because of the overpopulation problem.

Puppy Mills and Pet Stores

Most dogs sold in pet shops—more than 400,000 a year—come from breeding kennels called "puppy mills." Many are located in Kansas, Arkansas, Iowa, Missouri, Nebraska, Oklahoma, and Pennsylvania, but they can be found in other states as well. These kennels breed as many puppies as they can as rapidly as possible. Female dogs live in crowded outdoor cages where they are bred continuously, with no rest between litters. Mothers and their puppies suffer from malnutrition, disease, exposure, and lack of veterinary care. After the mother's puppies are taken away from her, she becomes pregnant again so she can give birth to more puppies.

Puppy mills sell these puppies to dealers who in turn pack them in crates and ship them off to pet stores. The crated puppies are often forced to travel hundreds of miles by truck, tractor trailer, or even plane. Many get sick without adequate food, water, or ventilation and some die. Because of being taken away from their mothers early and transported to a pet store, the dogs often suffer serious emotional and physical problems.

Puppy kennels are supposed to be licensed, but often they aren't. The U.S. Department of Agriculture has the responsibility of regulating puppy mills, but it is too overworked and understaffed to do its job properly. Most kennels never get inspected. Those that are, often have substandard conditions. When a female dog is too old, sick, or worn out to have more puppies, her usefulness is over. Often she is taken away and shot. Cat breeding for profit also exists, but on a much smaller scale.

Life in a pet shop isn't much of an improvement. The puppy who survives her trip from the breeding kennel to the pet shop must often endure cramped and unsanitary conditions without adequate veterinary care once she gets there. As a result, pet shops often end up selling sick or injured animals to the public. In addition, there are no laws that regulate how pet stores should dispose of their animals. Many stores kill sick or unwanted animals they can't sell. They then may put their bodies out with the trash.

As more people become aware of the pet overpopulation problem, they are less willing to get their pets from breeders who raise animals for profit and from pet stores. In some parts of the country the puppy mill business is hurting. Breeders and puppy mill owners are complaining about the drop in prices and the reduction in puppy orders.

Pound Seizure

The term "pound seizure" refers to the practice of releasing and selling unclaimed cats and dogs from animal shelters for use in biomedical research, product testing, and medical and hospital training. Five states (Iowa, Minnesota, Oklahoma, South Dakota, and Utah) have pound-seizure laws that require public animal shelters (also called pounds) to release and sell their animals to individuals or institutions that would use them in experimentation and research. Fourteen states have laws that forbid pound seizure. The remaining states either have a law allowing researchers to use animals from public shelters under certain conditions or have no law at all. In states without any law the shelters decide for themselves whether or not they want to release their animals.[2]

As a result of these pound seizure laws, 200,000 stray cats and dogs die in experiments and teaching labs each year. Animal researchers say these unwanted animals would be killed anyway, so it is better that they die in a way that helps science. The problem is that oftentimes research labs get the shelter animals who are the healthiest and the easiest to handle, and these are the ones who would most likely be chosen for adoption.

3
ANIMALS IN EDUCATION

American education uses five to six million animals each year, from preschool to graduate school. The animals are utilized for educational purposes, either as classroom pets at the elementary level or as objects of vivisection at the graduate school level.

Science projects and fairs sometimes employ tests or even surgery on animals. In most secondary school biology classes dissection is a laboratory requirement. College and graduate school psychology classes use animals in experiments. American medical and veterinary schools use animal labs to teach physiology and surgery. About 50,000 animals, mostly dogs, are used each year to teach medical and veterinary students, although a growing number of medical schools have dropped animal labs or allow their students non-animal alternatives.

Animals in the Classroom

A student's first encounter with animals in school is most likely with such classroom pets as hamsters, gerbils, guinea pigs, rabbits, lizards, turtles, birds, or fish. The experience can be an enriching one for students, especially city children, who may have little contact with animals. Classroom pets can teach compassion for animals and respect for life.

In elementary school pupils sometimes get to see how chicks are born. The fertile eggs are incubated and hatched in the classroom. However, since a classroom is no place for growing chickens, they are usually sent off to a nearby chicken farm. Students may or may not be aware that the cute chicks they watched grow will end up becoming chickens to be used for food.

Jenifer Graham

In 1987, 15-year-old Jenifer Graham got into trouble for refusing to dissect a frog in biology class. She was a tenth-grader at Victor Valley High School in Victorville, California. In March when it came time for the frog dissection, Jenifer asked her teacher for permission to do another assignment. She felt she could learn about a frog's anatomy without dissecting one. The teacher turned down Jenifer's request. He told her that if she didn't dissect the frog she would get an F in the course.

The teacher sent Jenifer to see the principal. She explained to the principal as best she could her strong

Jenifer Graham was a tenth-grade student in California in 1987 when she refused to dissect a frog in her biology class. As a result of her stand, California became the first state in the nation to grant its students the right to choose an alternative to dissection.

beliefs against the unnecessary killing of animals. She asked the principal if there wasn't an alternate assignment she could do. It wasn't as if she was looking to get out of any work. She just wanted her beliefs respected.

Jenifer went home discouraged. She loved biology. It was important to her that she do well in the subject, especially since she was already thinking about becoming a marine biologist. She didn't want to fail biology, but she didn't want to go against her conscience either.

Jenifer's mother, Pat Graham, sought help for her daughter from the Humane Society of the United States (HSUS), an animal welfare organization in Washington, D.C. The society contacted the school with a list of alternatives, but the school refused to compromise. HSUS attorneys filed suit in federal district court against the school board to defend Jenifer's right to follow her conscience. Their argument was that the first amendment protection of religious freedom covered Jenifer's right to refuse dissection on ethical grounds. What began as a local controversy became a national issue when Jenifer appeared on a national talk show to tell her story. Many people were impressed by her courageous stand.

Soon afterwards Jenifer testified before a committee of the state legislature. She spoke in favor of a student rights bill that would let California students decide for themselves whether or not they want to dissect animals. Elementary and secondary students opposed to dissection on moral grounds were to be given alternative lessons. The state legislature passed the bill, and in March, 1988, the governor of California signed it into law. Jenifer's story received more national attention on October 17, 1989, when CBS broadcast "Frog Girl: The Jenifer Graham Story" as an afternoon TV special.

The legal case dragged on in the courts for several years, but in the end Jenifer was victorious. The court ordered that the negative remarks about Jenifer's refusal to do dissection be removed from her school transcript. It also ordered that documents relating to the independent tutorial she took to supplement her biology course work be added, including the A she received for it. The court ordered the school board to pay Jenifer's legal expenses.

The Dissection Controversy

Biology, anatomy, and physiology classes generally include the dissection of animals as part of their course requirements. Dissection animals include worms, hamsters, mice, rats, gerbils, fetal pigs, frogs, and cats. Biological supply companies sell and deliver the animals to the schools. Some of the animals they supply are "preserved specimens," which means they are killed ahead of time.

The other animals are either dissected alive, or they are killed before the dissection at the school by suffocation, drowning, carbon dioxide gas poisoning, or most commonly, a blow to the back of the neck. Frogs are "pithed"

These frogs are two of the hundreds of thousands of frogs dissected in American classrooms every year.

in the classroom. Pithing involves inserting a small, metal rod into the frog to sever its spinal cord.

The animals can suffer mistreatment at the hands of the biological supply companies that supply animals for dissection, since these companies tend to cage, kill, and transport the animals as cheaply as possible. There is also concern about the disappearance of frogs from their natural habitats in many parts of the world. Many frogs are caught in the wild before they are transported to the supply company and then on to the school for dissection. Even frog breeders restock their populations by capturing frogs in the wild.

Proponents of dissection defend the educational value of dissecting animal specimens in the classroom. Dr. Adrian Morrison, director of the Office of Animal Research Issues at the Alcohol, Drug Abuse, and Mental Health Administration in Rockville, Maryland, says that "dissection gives students a unique opportunity to observe how animals are structured to function the way they do."[1] Not only will students better appreciate the workings of living organisms, he claims, but learning about the intricacies of animal anatomy will help them understand how organisms have evolved through the centuries.

Critics of dissection say biology, which means "the study of life," should teach respect for life, not its destruction. Why do students need to cut up animals to learn biology anyway, they ask. After all, students learn about human anatomy without cutting up human beings.

Moreover, having to cut up animals can be an upsetting and psychologically harmful experience for students. Dr. Eric Dunayer, V.M.D., director of Alternatives in Education and Research for the Association of Veterinarians for Animal Rights, says, "Dissection is an archaic practice easily replaced by modern and educationally sound alternatives."

A number of educators are questioning the necessity of dissection, and some teachers are modifying their courses. A biology textbook published by Holt Rinehart Winston replaces required dissections with safe experiments on live animals.[2] Teachers who use plastic models, transparent overlays, videotapes, and computer programs claim these alternatives not only teach anatomy better, but students can use them as many times as they want to learn the lesson. While some alternatives can be expensive, they usually turn out to be cost-effective in the long run.

Supporters of dissection claim that there is no substitute for students seeing and feeling for themselves the actual parts of a dissected animal. Dissection is a simple, direct, and effective non-textbook teaching tool, they say, that allows a student to experience what it is to be a scientist—to observe, think, question, and test.

The controversy places many teachers and school officials in a difficult position. They are expected to uphold traditional educational methods and established curricula while at the same time respecting the feelings and beliefs of students and parents opposed to dissection. Most teachers try to be sensitive to student concerns about this issue,

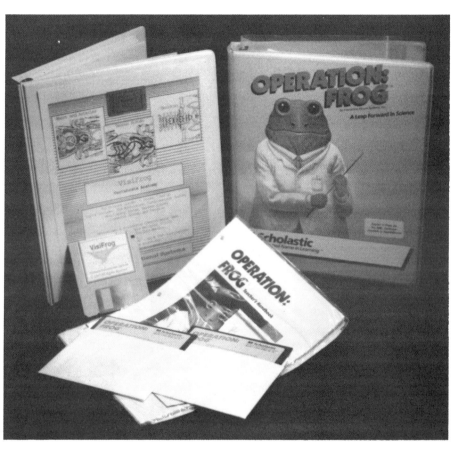

These two computer programs—"VisiFrog" and "Operation: Frog"—are among the growing number of alternatives to dissection now available to students.

but some teachers have been known to pressure students, to perform dissections against their will.[3]

After her daughter's story received national attention in the late 1980s, Pat Graham received so many calls from students and parents asking for advice that she set up a toll-free dissection hotline (1-800-922-FROG) with the help of the Animal Legal Defense Fund. Since 1989, the hotline has received more than 50,000 calls.[4]

One typical call came from an Illinois high school sophomore. She was threatened with a lowered grade in her biology class when she refused—on ethical grounds—to dissect an earthworm. "I don't feel it's right to harm any animals just for a grade," she said. "I don't care if it is an earthworm. They have as much right to live as we do."[5]

Thanks to Jenifer Graham, California became the first state in the nation to grant its students the right to choose an alternative to dissection. Florida became the second state, and Maine followed by adopting a statewide policy that gives its students a choice. Rhode Island is just one of a number of other states that are considering similar legislation.

In the summer of 1992 Pennsylvania became the fourth state in the nation to offer its students an alternative when Governor Robert Casey signed a law that guarantees a non-animal choice to all Pennsylvania students in grades K-12 who have sincere objections to participating in dissection. "I'm so relieved that no one will ever have to face what I had to face," said Dawn Leedie, a recent graduate of Springfield High School who was required to dissect a monkey in her junior year. "It's about time!"[6]

Some countries have stopped the practice altogether. Argentina removed dissection from its schools on the grounds that "biology is the science of life, and it is not consistent to teach it at the expense of the death of other beings . . . experiments on animals are part of a dangerous process which tends to desensitize the mind to pain, to suffering, to respect and to life itself."

Two major national teacher groups have addressed the issue. In 1990 the National Science Teachers Association (NSTA) endorsed the use of animals in the classroom on the grounds that "observation and experimentation with organisms give students unique perspectives of life processes that are not provided by other modes of instruction." However, the group advised its members to consider "student views or beliefs sensitive to dissection."

In 1989 the National Association of Biology Teachers (NABT) published a new policy which states that "all biology teachers should foster a respect for life" and that "NABT is commited to providing teachers' materials that offer alternatives to the more traditional practices involving dissection and vivisection." The group declared dissection permissible "provided no student is forced to participate over his or her objections."[7]

Medical and Veterinary Education

Most medical schools use animals in their education. Although dogs, cats, and sometimes even horses and cows have been used to teach physiology and the effects of drugs on the heart, dogs are commonly used to teach students surgical skills. The dogs used in these teaching labs come from animal dealers, companies which breed and sell dogs to research facilities, and shelters.

After the dogs are anesthetized students cut them open and practice surgery on their bodies. Students sew the dogs back up after the lesson is over. When the dog recovers, he or she may be used again. When their usefulness is over, they are euthanized.

Those critical of using live, healthy animals to practice surgery do not believe it is the best training for performing surgery on humans. They think serving an apprenticeship under an experienced surgeon the way medical students in other countries do is better preparation. Britain halted the use of live animals in medical education more than 100 years ago. British surgeons learn their surgical skills by observing operations by senior surgeons, practicing on human cadavers, and then by operating on live humans under close supervision. It is illegal in Britain for medical students to practice surgery on animals.

While the medical school professors who insist on animal labs say that practice surgery on live animals is good training, many medical schools permit their students to choose non-animal alternatives and a growing number of medical schools no longer use animal labs at all. By 1992 one-quarter of the medical schools in the United States—including Yale, Northwestern, Washington, Michigan, Ohio State, Maryland, Louisiana State, and New York University—had dropped animal labs from their curricula.

Veterinary schools also use live animals to train their students. The argument in favor of animal labs for veterinary training would seem to be stronger since veterinarians need to know how to treat sick and injured animals while medical doctors treat human beings.

In 1984 two students at the University of Pennsylvania School of Veterinary Medicine, Gloria Binkowski and Eric Dunayer, asked to be excused from the lab that would have required them to practice surgery on live, healthy dogs and then put them to death afterwards. The dean of the school and his staff informed the students they would be expelled if they refused to perform the practice surgery. When the students refused, they flunked the course. That meant they would not be able to continue their studies.

With legal help from several animal rights organizations the students took the university to court. Eventually they won their case, completed their studies, and graduated. Today Gloria and Eric are veterinarians, and the University of Pennsylvania School of Veterinary Medicine—as well as the veterinary schools of Tufts, Colorado State, and Michigan State—provides an alternative to students who want to train for their profession without harming healthy animals.[8]

Some veterinary schools, like Cornell and Washington State, have spay-and-return programs that allow their students to operate on dogs and cats from local shelters who need to be spayed and neutered. Not only do the operations help the animals by giving them a better chance of being adopted, but they provide students with valuable experience since spaying and neutering involve all the basic surgical skills. Young people who want to be veterinarians are increasingly being offered educationally sound alternatives that do not involve hurting animals.[9]

4

ANIMAL RESEARCH

Nobody knows for sure how many animals are destroyed in laboratories each year. Throughout the world the total is well over 200 million. In the United States the estimates range from 15 to 100 million animals, depending on who is doing the estimating. Animal research is a multi-billion dollar industry that involves over a thousand universities, hospitals, and research institutes across the country. More than 85 percent of the animals used in laboratories are mice and rats, but research labs also use cats, dogs, rabbits, reptiles, amphibians, cows, pigs, sheep, monkeys, and chimpanzees.

Animal research covers a wide range of activities—everything from biomedical research to psychology experiments, drug tests, addiction studies, cosmetics and household product tests, and military experiments.

American companies and commercial testing firms use animals to test lipstick, shampoo, deodorant, eye shadow, furniture polish, oven cleaners, pesticides, paints, glues, liquid office supplies, and even toys. General Motors uses live animals in its crash studies to test the safety of its new cars. U.S. Surgical Corporation, a medical supply company in Norwalk, Connecticut, with annual sales of more than $800 million, uses thousands of dogs each year to demonstrate the use of its surgical staplers.

Biomedical Research

Biomedical research uses animals to study living organisms, cure diseases, produce vaccines and antibodies, and refine surgical and organ transplant techniques. Just how important animals are for this research is the question that divides supporters and opponents of animal research.

Defenders of animal research maintain that most of the medical advances of the twentieth century, including vaccines for polio and measles, cancer chemotherapy, open-heart surgery, and insulin for diabetics, were made possible by laboratory research done on animals. They claim that about two-thirds of the Nobel prizes awarded for physiology or medicine since 1901 have been given for work that depended at least in part on animal research.[1]

These defenders say animal experiments need to continue if biomedical research is to combat such life-threatening diseases as cancer, heart disease, and AIDS.

According to the North Carolina Association for Biomedical Research, "laboratory animals provide one of the very best ways known to study the human body and diseases that afflict it." Moreover, say the supporters of animal research, many of the treatments developed for people with the help of animal research, such as antibiotics, blood transfusions, and organ transplants, benefit animals as well.[2]

On the other side of the debate are those who contend that animal research is wasteful, cruel, misleading, and unnecessary. They say claims made on behalf of animal research are greatly exaggerated. For example, defenders of animal research claim that people are living twenty years longer than they used to because of research using laboratory animals. However, medical historians say people are living longer primarily because of better sanitation and improved public health measures that have reduced the threat of such diseases as typhoid, small pox, whooping cough, and tuberculosis. These deadly diseases were already in decline by the time medical measures based on animal research were employed to treat them.

The truth about just how much animal research has contributed to medical progress is hard to assess because we cannot know what our health would be like today if scientists had decided to concentrate on non-animal research. Opponents of animal research point out that the massive destruction of animal life in research labs through the years has done little to combat cancer or heart disease.

These diseases kill millions of Americans every year. Some cancers, like breast cancer, are getting worse rather than better. Most doctors admit that the war against cancer has been a disappointment and more efforts are needed to prevent cancer before it begins.

Two physician groups—the Medical Research Modernization Committee and the Physicians Committee for Responsible Medicine—are critical of modern medicine's overdependence on animal research. These doctors believe animal research is wasteful and the billions of taxpayer dollars invested annually in it would be better spent on clinical research and public health programs. They disagree with the American Medical Association (AMA), which strongly supports animal research.[3]

Dr. Richard Weiskopf, an internist in Syracuse, New York, and a member of the Medical Research Modernization Committee, believes most current animal research is unnecessary. "As a physician, I am well aware of the excessive duplication in the medical literature," he says. "How many research projects that experiment on animals could be accomplished by other means, such as computer models, cell culture, human clinical investigation, epidemiology, non-invasive scanning or post-marketing drug surveillance?"

Dr. Weiskopf believes animal research "is severely limited by anatomical, physiological and pathological differences between people and non-human animals." That is why conclusions derived from animal research are

These two baby monkeys are part of an addiction study. They have been turned into drug addicts to study the effect of drugs on human beings.

so often misleading, he says. One of the examples he gives is the smoking tests that were done on dogs. For many years thousands of dogs were hooked up to machines that forced them to breathe cigarette smoke. Studies on humans had already revealed that cigarette smoking caused lung cancer. However, since the dogs didn't come down with lung cancer, the tests continued. Since the public was not warned about the dangers of smoking, many people died of lung cancer.[4]

Critics of animal research range from those who want to reform animal research to those who want to abolish it. Reformers want to minimize animal suffering through the "3Rs" approach. They want to *replace* animal experiments with non-animal alternatives wherever possible, *reduce* the number of animals used through more careful design of experiments, and *refine* procedures so that the animals experience less pain and suffering.

Abolitionists want to do away with animal research completely. They say the real question about animal research is not "Is it useful?" but "Is it right?" They ask if we humans have the right to raise, capture, cage, and kill animals simply because we might learn something. Do we have the right to force drugs and alcohol on animals to study the effects of those drugs? Is it right to give animals our diseases so we can try to find a cure for them? Abolitionists are not interested in cleaner cages. They want no cages at all.

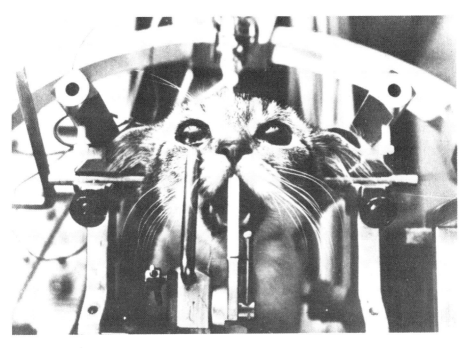

This stereotaxic instrument has immobilized a cat for an experiment by inserting bars into the cat's mouth and ear canals. Stereotaxic instruments are widely used in animal research.

While the search for non-animal alternatives and a growing public awareness will no doubt reduce the number of animals used in laboratories in the years ahead, animal research will continue for the foreseeable future. Most researchers welcome non-animal alternatives as valuable "adjuncts" to their work, but they maintain that many of the most important medical questions will only be answered by research on living organisms. They say non-animal alternatives cannot show what happens inside a brain, or how a new drug will affect the heart or nervous system.

Dr. A. Clifford Barger, president of the Massachusetts Society for Medical Research, warns, "While we continue to investigate and use techniques such as cell cultures and computer simulations that reduce the need for animals, animal research cannot be eliminated without drastic consequences for human and veterinary medicine."[5]

Product Testing

In the United States the government requires companies to test their products for safety before they are sold to the public. Most companies test their products on animals. They have been doing this for a long time to protect themselves against consumer lawsuits.

The most commonly used product safety test is the LD 50 Test. LD is an abbreviation for Lethal Dose, and 50 stands for the 50% of the animals who must die for the test to be complete. Today the LD 50 Test is part of the guidelines of almost every government regulatory agency for testing substances to be used in the United States and abroad. These substances include drugs, cosmetics, household products, food additives, and industrial and agricultural chemicals.

A typical LD 50 test involves poisoning up to 200 mice, rats, or guinea pigs. Dogs, rabbits, calves, and primates are also used, but less frequently. The most common LD 50 Test is the *oral LD 50*. In this test the substance is forced into the animal's stomach through a tube. Other methods involve inserting the test substance into the animal's lungs, injecting it into the body, or applying it to the skin. In these skin irritancy tests lab technicians apply chemicals to the shaved, raw skin of rabbits or other animals who have been locked into restraining devices.

These LD 50 tests, which can last for weeks, cause tremors, convulsions, comas, vomiting, diarrhea, paralysis, and bleeding from the eyes, nose, mouth, and rectum. The half of the test animals who survive are killed after the test is over.

The Draize Eye Irritancy Test is the standard test for products that might get into people's eyes. Dr. John Draize of the Food and Drug Administration (FDA) developed the test. It was adopted in 1938 as the standard test for measuring eye irritancy in cosmetics, chemicals, drugs, pesticides, and household products such as paints, oven cleaners, and dish detergents.

In a typical Draize Test, six to 18 rabbits are locked into wooden stocks so they can't move. A lab technician then

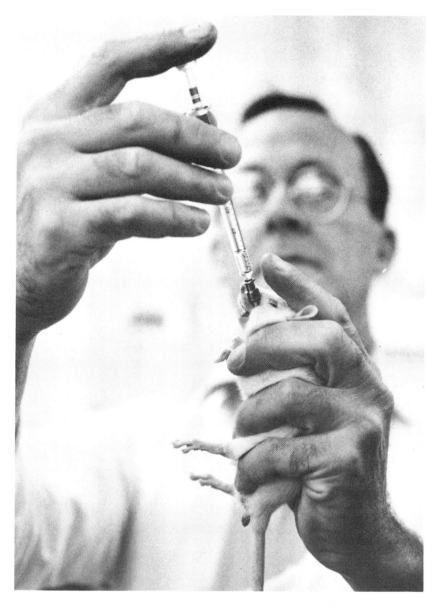

This lab scientist is injecting a white mouse with a test substance in a
Lethal Dose-50 Test. Most American companies test their products on
animals before putting them on the market.

drops, places, or sprays the test substance into one of the rabbit's eyes. Rabbits are preferred for this test because they have no tear ducts to create tears that will wash the test substance away.

Technicians inspect the damage at intervals of 1, 24, 48, 72, and 168 hours and record the results. Damage to the rabbit's eye ranges from redness and swelling to severe ulceration, hemorrhage, and blindness. After the test is over rabbits are often used again for another test like the skin irritancy test before they are killed.

Thanks to protests and pressure from animal rights groups, Revlon, Avon, Benetton, Estée Lauder, and some other cosmetics companies stopped testing their products on animals. As a result of an increasing demand for cosmetics that are not tested on animals, the industry's use of the Draize Test fell by 87% in the 1980s.

The move away from animal testing appears to be gaining momentum as more companies turn to such non-animal alternatives as cell and organ cultures, placenta analysis, and computer and mathematical models. Still, many large companies like Bristol-Myers Squibb, Colgate-Palmolive, Gillette, Johnson & Johnson, L'Oréal, and Proctor & Gamble continue to test their products on animals.

Former U.S. Surgeon General Dr. C. Everett Koop defends the continuation of product testing on animals. At a news conference in Washington, D.C., on April 19, 1991, he said, "There is no substitute for animal testing if we are to ensure the safety of all consumer products, from personal care and household cleaning products to health care and prescription drugs."[6]

American companies have an incentive to switch to non-animal tests now that animal rights groups across the country are monitoring their policies and practices. These groups advise their members to avoid products from companies that test on animals and only buy from companies that are "cruelty-free."[7]

The Silver Spring Monkeys

The issue of the treatment of animals in research labs came to the attention of the public in 1981 when a 23-year-old college student by the name of Alex Pacheco reported on conditions at a research facility in Silver Spring, Maryland.

Pacheco was already an animal activist when in the spring of 1981 he decided he wanted firsthand experience in a research laboratory. He applied for and was accepted as a volunteer worker at the Institute for Behavioral Research (IBR), located not far from where he lived.

When he arrived on his first day, the director of the laboratory, Dr. Edward Taub, gave him a tour. The offices in the front of the institute looked normal enough. However, as soon as they walked through the doors into the back, Pacheco knew something was wrong:

> The smell was incredible . . . I saw filth caked on the wires of the cages, feces piled in the bottom of the cages, urine and rust encrusting every surface. There, amid this

rotting stench sat seventeen monkeys, their lives limited to metal boxes just 17 3/4 inches wide . . . they were picking forlornly at scraps and fragments of broken biscuits that had fallen through the wire. . . . There were no dishes to keep the food away from the feces, nothing for the animals to sit on but the jagged wires of the old cages, nothing for them to see but the filthy, feces-splattered walls of that windowless room.[8]

Pacheco found out that 12 of the 17 monkeys had disabled limbs as a result of surgery that severed their nerves when they were juveniles. The purpose of the research was to monitor "the rehabilitation of impaired limbs." He learned that eight-year-old Sarah had lived alone in her cage since she was one day old. The operating room where Dr. Taub and his colleagues surgically crippled the monkeys was filthy—old shoes, dirty clothes, urine stains, rat droppings, and cockroaches, living and dead, were all over the room.

Pacheco took careful notes of everything he observed. When he was there alone at night and on weekends, he took photographs of the monkeys, cages, restraining chairs, surgery room, and the blood on the floors. He found on Dr. Taub's desk in his office a monkey skull and a surgically removed monkey hand, complete with fur, nails, and skin. Pacheco brought five primate experts, including a doctor and a veterinarian, to the lab at night to see the conditions for themselves.

When he felt he had enough evidence, Pacheco went to the police. He turned over all his notes and photographs,

This Silver Spring monkey is in a restraining device called a "primate chair." For this experiment researchers at the Institute of Behavioral Research in Maryland severed the spinal cords of the monkeys and surgically crippled their arms.

his own sworn statement about conditions in the lab, and the sworn testimony of the primate experts. On September 11, 1981, the police raided the institute. It was the first police raid on a research laboratory in American history.

The state of Maryland charged Dr. Taub with seventeen counts of cruelty against the monkeys (one for each monkey). The publicity caused the National Institutes of Health (NIH) to suspend its government funding of Dr. Taub's research.

After a jury found Taub guilty on six counts, his lawyers appealed the verdict and were granted a second trial. The new jury found him guilty on one count of cruelty. When Taub and his team of lawyers appealed to the Maryland Court of Appeals, the state's highest court threw out his conviction on a technicality. The court ruled that researchers funded by the federal government were not subject to the state's anti-cruelty law.

Even though in the end Dr. Taub was not convicted, the case brought the issue of animal research to the attention of the public. For the first time in American history a researcher had been charged with cruelty to animals in a laboratory.

Animal Welfare Act

Public concern about the Silver Spring monkeys put pressure on the government to strengthen the Animal Welfare Act. The act, first passed by Congress in 1966, required animal dealers and research laboratories to be licensed. The act was amended in 1970 and 1976 to establish minimum animal care standards. The law stated that primates, cats, dogs, rabbits, guinea pigs, and hamsters were to be provided with proper cages, food, water, and sanitation. However, the regulations drawn up to enforce the law exempted mice, rats, and birds, which comprise the vast majority of animals used in testing and research.

Although the Animal Welfare Act requires that researchers use anesthetics on the lab animals covered by the law, it allows researchers to withhold pain killers "when scientifically necessary." Because of these loopholes and inadequate funding, animal advocates say the act is ineffective.

When the Silver Spring monkey case created pressure for more reforms, the Animal Welfare Act was amended again in 1985. The U.S. Department of Agriculture was called on to establish new regulations to improve the condition of lab animals. Research labs were supposed to promote the "psychological well-being" of their captive monkeys and other primates.

They were also supposed to provide better treatment for dogs. Dogs were to be kept in compatible groups unless research required them to be kept in a single cage. Dogs housed in laboratories were supposed to be taken out of their cages and given a walk. Research institutions complained that these new regulations would cost millions of dollars, which may be why the regulations have not been fully implemented.

In 1990 an attempt was made to expand the coverage of the Animal Welfare Act. The Humane Society of the

United States (HSUS) and the Animal Legal Defense Fund (ALDF) filed a lawsuit against the U.S. Department of Agriculture. The USDA had denied their petition to extend legal protection to rats, mice, and birds because it would cost too much.

On January 8, 1991, U.S. District Judge Charles Richey ruled that rats, mice, and birds should be covered by the Animal Welfare Act. Their exclusion, he said, sends a message "that the researchers may subject the birds, rats, and mice to cruel and inhumane conditions, that such conduct is sanctioned by the government and has no legal consequences."[9]

Biomedical researchers claim they treat laboratory animals humanely and abide by the federal regulations that govern their use. "Scientists, veterinarians, physicians, surgeons, and others who do research in animal laboratories are as much concerned about the care of animals as anyone can be," says Dr. Michael DeBakey, heart specialist and chancellor of the Baylor College of Medicine in Houston, Texas. "Their respect for the dignity of life and compassion for the sick and disabled, in fact, is what motivated them to search for ways of relieving the pain and suffering caused by diseases."[10]

5
THE ANIMALS WE EAT

In early America farmers not only fed themselves and their families, but they also supplied food to the artisans, merchants, and shopkeepers in the towns. As the country became more industrial and waves of immigrants arrived, a larger population had to be fed. With the growth of the suburbs after World War II even more people had to be provided with food.

It is a credit to the efficiency of modern agriculture that American farmers, who are about 2% of the population, are able to feed the entire country. As a result of research conducted at agricultural departments of universities and scientific institutes, new and more efficient methods of raising food animals have made American agriculture the envy of the world.

In earlier times farm animals got to spend most of their time outdoors. Storybooks still show this picture of healthy, happy farm animals enjoying the affectionate care of humans—cows grazing in a pasture, pigs rolling in the mud, chickens darting about the barnyard flapping their wings and scratching the ground for worms and insects.

However, modern farming is very different from what it used to be. Today's large corporate farms are not places where the six billion farm animals raised for food each year have much of a life. The meat and diary industries call this modern method of raising farm animals intensive livestock production, but the assembly-line nature of the method has caused others to call it "factory farming."

Peter Singer's book, *Animal Liberation,* provided many readers with their first look at the way animals are treated on today's factory farms. Since these large farms are now owned by corporations rather than individual farmers, they produce meat, eggs, and milk as quickly and as efficiently as possible. The small family farm is fast becoming a thing of the past.

Most of today's cows, calves, pigs, and chickens are raised indoors where they are subject to overcrowding, stress, physical mutilations, and drugs. Farm animals forced to spend their lives in crates and cages suffer from isolation and boredom as well.

When Singer's book was published in 1975, there were no groups paying much attention to the plight of farm animals. However, since that time some organizations—

such as Farm Animal Reform Movement (FARM), Food Animals Concerns Trust (FACT), Farm Sanctuary, and the Humane Farming Association—have been trying to educate the public.

Poultry

The transition from traditional family farming to modern factory farming started after World War II when large corporations began gaining control of poultry production. Today 50 big corporations control the American poultry industry, which produces about five billion chickens each year. Since family farms have difficulty competing with these corporations, the smaller farms have been forced to go out of business. Oil and other corporations not connected to agriculture have gone into farming to diversify their product line and gain tax advantages.

Broiler chickens. The mass production of chickens raised to be eaten—called broiler chickens—began in Delaware back in 1923 when Mrs. Wilmer Steele succeeded in raising the first flocks of chickens indoors in the winter. She discovered that when vitamins A and D were added to the chickens' feed, sunlight and exercise were no longer needed. However, it was not until after World War II that today's broad-breasted broiler chicken was developed and drugs and antibiotics were found that promoted growth and curbed disease.[1]

In today's highly successful multi-billion dollar broiler industry, chickens live in large windowless buildings that can hold up to 80,000 chickens. The broiler industry has decided on the most profitable density—each chicken is allowed about a half a foot of floor space. The chickens are debeaked to prevent them from pecking each other to death. It takes only seven weeks for broiler chickens to reach their market weight of about $3^1/_2$ pounds. The first and last time the chickens see daylight and breathe fresh air is the day they are packed into crates, loaded on trucks, and shipped to slaughter. When they arrive, workers remove the chickens from their crates and hang them upside down by their legs on a conveyor belt that takes them to their death.

Layer hens. Today 280 million factory-farm hens supply more than 95% of America's eggs. At the age of 18 weeks the debeaked hens are put in small wire cages—five or six hens per cage. The long rows of cages are stacked three or four levels high in large windowless buildings. The cages are tilted so that the eggs roll out onto a conveyor belt that takes them to be cleaned and packaged.

Dairy and Meat

Cows. The modern dairy industry is also becoming more mechanized. Traditional farmers used to milk their cows by hand. On today's large corporate farms about half the nation's 10 million dairy cows are milked by machine three

These hens are so crowded in their cages they cannot spread their wings. Their beaks have been cut off to prevent them from injuring each other. The eggs they lay are taken away by conveyor belt.

times a day around the clock. The cows are fed hormones to make them produce as much milk as possible. They are also injected with antibiotics to treat mastitis, a mammary gland infection that afflicts about half of America's dairy cows, according to the U.S. Department of Agriculture.[2]

Cow's milk is meant for calves, but calves are taken away from their mother shortly after birth so the farmer will have ten months worth of milk to sell. After the milk supply starts to dry up, then the cow is made pregnant again so more milk is available to the farmer. By keeping the cow continuously pregnant, the farmer is assured of a steady supply of milk. Normally a cow would live twenty years or more. However, factory-farm cows only produce milk for a few years, after which they are sent to slaughter.

Calves. The dairy farmer gets to use the calves that are born to his cows. The female calves grow up to be dairy cows, while male calves are raised for their meat (veal). Animal advocates regard veal production as especially cruel. A young veal calf spends his life in a narrow crate (22" wide) standing on a slatted wooden floor, often in his own excrement. Calves are fed a substitute milk diet purposely deficient in iron to make them anemic so their flesh will be tender. They are not given straw bedding for fear they will get the iron their bodies need by eating the straw. Calves are also given drugs and antibiotics twice a day. About half of the antibiotics produced in this country are fed to farm animals.

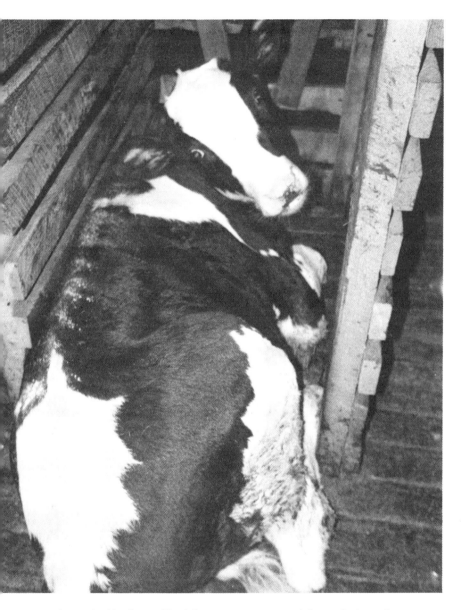

This veal calf will spend his life in a narrow crate with his neck chained so he can't turn around. Veal calves are kept purposely anemic so their flesh will be tender when they are slaughtered.

After four months the veal calves reach their market weight. Some calves are so weak and shaky on their feet they have to be dragged to the truck that will take them to the slaughterhouse. England banned the veal crate in 1990. In this country many animal advocates have asked people not to buy or eat veal. The public seems to be responding. Veal consumption has fallen by 70% in recent years.

Cattle. Beef cattle spend the first six months or so of their lives in pastures. Then most are transported to enclosed outdoor areas called feedlots. There they are fattened up on grain for the last 100 days of their lives until they reach a market weight of about 1,000 pounds. They are denied their natural high-fiber diet of grass and hay, which would slow down their weight gain. To counteract their unhealthy diet, they also must be given antibiotics.

Pigs. A growing percentage of the 55 million pigs reared for food in the United States each year come from farms where the pigs are raised indoors and are provided with only a few square feet of space. The breeding sows (female pigs) are kept confined in stalls with slatted concrete floors. After the piglets they produce are taken away from them after eight weeks, the sows are impregnated again.

Livestock Transportation

Each year millions of farm animals die on their way to slaughter. With little protection from the weather on trucks that criss-cross the country animals suffer from hunger, thirst, and overcrowding. Some trips can last up to 60 hours. Cattle and other farms animals denied food and water often contract a disease called shipping fever.

According to a federal law that applies to the transportation of livestock, livestock must be taken off the vehicle to be fed, watered, and allowed to rest every 28 hours. However, the 28-Hour Law only applies to train and ship transport—not to trucks. Since only 5% of farm animals travel by train or ship, that leaves 95% of the six billion farm animals transported to slaughter each year not covered by the law.

When farm animals arrive at stockyards and auction houses, they are usually weak, hungry, and thirsty. Veal calves and pigs who were never allowed to walk have an especially difficult time. Workers get the animals off the trucks by poking them with electric prods. On their way down slippery ramps many animals fall, break bones, and get trampled. Animals that fall and are too weak or injured to get back up are called "downers." Workers either drag them out of the way or leave them where they fall. Later they may be dragged through the stockyard to a "dead pile," or they may be put on a truck with other downers and driven there. If they are still alive, they may be slaughtered for food.

Although the meat industry loses millions of dollars every year from livestock lost in transit, the industry says that transporting farm animals more humanely would

At stockyards, animals too sick or injured to walk are called "downers." These two downed cows will either be dragged to a "dead pile" or to slaughter if they are still alive.

increase costs and result in higher food prices for the consumer.

The Factory Farming Controversy

The meat industry says animal advocates are misleading the public about the way farm animals are treated. They say no one cares more about the health and well-being of farm animals than farmers. According to the Animal Industry Foundation, "One of the best strongholds of animal welfare in our culture is the farmer. It is in the farmer's own best interest to see the animals in his charge treated humanely, guaranteeing him a healthy, high quality animal, a greater return on his investment, and a wholesome food product." [3]

Defenders of modern farming methods also say that farm animals are fed better now than they were in the past. Before, pigs might have been fed household scraps or spoiled food, but today the pigs have special diets that make them grow faster. Moreover, they say, farm animals are better off indoors where they are protected from weather extremes and where the temperature and ventilation can be controlled more easily. The meat and dairy industries also defend their practice of confining animals in cages and stalls. They say keeping farm animals confined protects the weaker ones from the stronger.

Critics of modern intensive livestock-growing methods say that factory farming is not only bad for animals, but it's bad for the environment too. Since there are no sewage systems for farm animals, millions of tons of manure pollute the land, water, and air. Livestock manure releases huge amounts of methane gas into the air, and the drugs and chemicals that farm animals eat get washed into the soil and into nearby lakes and streams.

From one-third to one-half of the world's grain goes to feed livestock, but in the United States the figure is even higher. Seventy percent of the corn, oats, soybeans, and other grains we grow goes to feed our livestock. Some people say it would be better—and healthier too—if that grain went directly to people. It is estimated that half the grain we use to feed our cattle and other livestock would feed all the hungry people in the world.

Critics also point out that the world's livestock industry destroys rain forests. Millions of trees have been cut down to create grazing land for cattle and for the growing of the grain needed to feed them. Rain forests around the world are being destroyed at an alarming rate so cattle can be raised and slaughtered for meat. This destruction causes erosion, soil depletion, and damage to the ozone layer. It may also contribute to global warming.

Alternatives

People opposed to factory farming out of their concern for animal suffering, the environment, and human health often look for alternatives. Some prefer to buy their meat, milk, eggs, and cheese at health or natural food stores. These stores offer organic and free-range produce from farms where farm animals live outdoors, are treated more humanely, and are free of the drugs and hormones factory farms feed their animals.

People looking for alternatives to factory-farm produce also look for farmer markets or food co-ops supplied by small farms. Or they may purchase their food directly from local farms. The food may cost more, but its quality is usually better than factory-farmed supermarket food. Buying food locally also helps small farms stay in business.

Some people choose to eat no meat at all. Medical researchers are now generally agreed that animal fat is a major cause of cancer and heart disease. That is why the American Heart Association recommends a low-fat diet that's rich in fruits, vegetables, and grains and avoids the saturated fats found in meat, butter, cheese, cream, and whole milk. People are now eating less meat per capita than they used to. For example, beef consumption is down 30% in recent years.

People who avoid eating animal flesh—meat, poultry, fish, and other sea food—are called *vegetarians*. Vegetarians eat fruits, vegetables, grains, nuts, beans, and other plant foods instead of meat. Vegetarians who consume no milk, cheese, butter, and any other animal product are called *vegans*. A well-balanced vegetarian diet not only provides sufficient protein, vitamins, and minerals, but it keeps out of the body animal fat that has been linked to diseases.

Today there are approximately twelve million vegetarians in the United States (4 to 5 percent of the population). That's about two million more than ten years ago.[4]

Many vegans also try to avoid wearing anything that comes from an animal—like leather, fur, wool, down, or silk. They believe that killing animals for food, clothing, or any other reason is wrong.[5]

6

HUNTING, TRAPPING, AND ENTERTAINMENT

Before the 1992 Summer Olympics in Barcelona, there were several protests against bullfighting in Spain. The protesters said that Spanish bullfights torment bulls for entertainment. Before the event the bull's horns are shaved and the bull is weakened with laxatives so he is less able to defend himself. The bull becomes frightened and confused when he is forced into the arena. The bull is stabbed repeatedly in the course of the bullfight and becomes helpless from the loss of so much blood. The finale of the event takes place before a cheering crowd when the matador finally kills the bull.

The protesters also drew attention to other forms of animal abuse at Spanish fiestas. These include tormenting bulls and cows with metal-tipped sticks and throwing live goats to their deaths from church bell towers.

Spain is but one of the countries where animals are used in sports and entertainment. Throughout the world there is hunting, trapping, fishing, carriage and pony rides, horse and dog racing, rodeos, circuses, staged animal fights, and the use of animals in movies and television. Mohandas K. Gandhi, the founder of modern India, said, "The greatness of a nation and its moral progress can be judged by the way its animals are treated."[1]

Hunting

American hunters kill more than 250 million animals each year with rifles, shotguns, handguns, and bows and arrows. That is about one animal killed for every man, woman, and child in the United States. That figure doesn't include the millions of other animals that hunters have crippled or maimed. For every animal hunters kill, at least two more are wounded. Wounded animals often die from loss of blood, infection, and starvation.

Hunters—especially deer hunters—say they are helping control animal populations. Since natural predators like wolves and large cats are increasingly rare, humans must take the place of the predators and thin the herds, they say. Hunters also claim that animals killed by weapons suffer less than animals who die of disease or starvation.

Opponents of hunting point out there is a big difference between an Eskimo who must hunt to survive and a person who hunts for sport. They also deny that animals in the wild need humans to reduce their numbers. Nor do they believe hunters are really interested in reducing animal suffering. They say hunters go into the woods for only one reason—to kill animals.

Government wildlife officials promote pro-hunter policies when they increase the number of deer and other game animals on state and federally owned lands. These policies often involve the razing and burning of public land that is home to wildlife. That means bird watchers and other nature lovers who prefer to watch animals rather than shoot them lose out. Owls, woodpeckers, and hundreds of other non-game species are becoming rare or extinct. It has been suggested that wildlife officials maintain high levels of game animals so that they can profit from the sale of licenses hunters must purchase to shoot them.

Hunted animals aren't the only ones at risk. Hunters have been known to kill dogs, horses, cows, and even people. Each year hunting accidents take the lives of at least 200 Americans and injure about 2,000 others. Some of the people who have been shot were walking through the woods or on their own property. Many of the victims have been children. When hunting season opens, some people purposely keep their children and dogs away from the woods. Hunters themselves have the most to fear since most hunting accidents happen to them.

Some opponents of hunting engage in "hunt sabo- tages." They will go out into the woods with the hunters or ahead of them to warn the animals. Or on the day before

This hunter is holding the fowl he shot—two ducks in his right hand and a Canada goose in his left.

hunting season opens they might go into the woods and play loud radios or shoot in the air to make the animals more suspicious of humans. Since much hunting is done on private land, opponents encourage landowners to post NO HUNTING signs.

Some people say fishing is cruel, too. They point out that fish have sensitive nerve endings in their mouths that cause them pain when they are hooked. When fish are removed from the water, they suffocate because they can't breathe out of the water. Opponents of fishing say that if a fish could cry out like other animals do, people would be more aware of their suffering.

Hunting Ranches and Bird Shoots

Most hunters go into the woods and forests to shoot animals, but in "canned hunts" the animals are brought to the shooters. In the United States there are more than 4,000 hunting ranches (also called game ranches) where for a fee people can shoot animals. Hunting ranch managers purchase the animals (lions, tigers, and panthers are favorites) and bring them to their ranches for their customers.

Most of the time these "wild animals" have already been tamed and had their teeth and claws removed. The animal is brought in a cage to the shooting site, where the hunters are lined up. When the cage is opened, the animal either leaves on its own or is forced out. The hunters then open fire at close range. For extra money the slain animal can be mounted and taken home as a trophy.

Most of the animals shot at these game ranches are surplus zoo animals or the offspring of zoo animals. Others come from circuses, traveling animal acts, petting zoos, and other places where they are no longer needed.

There are also bird shoots where pigeons, ducks, pheasants, chickens, or turkeys are brought to an open area in boxes and released. England banned these bird shoots in 1921. In the United States they are legal in five states.

Every Labor Day one of the largest bird shoots in the world takes place in Hegins, Pennsylvania. The shoot—called the Fred Coleman Memorial Pigeon Shoot—has been held every year since 1934. Some of the pigeons are raised just for the shoot, but others are captured in cities and brought to Hegins. About 6,000 pigeons must be gathered for the event.

The pigeons are kept in crates for days and even weeks before the shoot, often with insufficient food or water. When Labor Day arrives, the pigeons are taken to the park where shooters pay a fee to enter the shoot. Boys from the town, called "trapper boys," take the pigeons from the crates and place them inside a row of small boxes on the field. Each box has a catapult inside. When the shooter yells "pull," the box is opened by a string and the catapult tosses the pigeon in the air.

The pigeons don't know where they are or where to go. Some have never flown before. Other pigeons from the city are used to people so they don't fly off right away. Some of the pigeons are too sick or injured to fly. The pigeons who don't fly away are shot on the ground.

The trapper boys, some as young as ten years old, run out and clear the field of pigeons. They either wring the necks of the wounded ones, or bring them back and put them alive in large bags that will hold them until they can be ground up for fertilizer. The shoot lasts all day. Families picnic in the park. When a pigeon is shot, people cheer.

There used to be a holiday mood at the shoot, but that has changed in recent years as a growing number of animal activists have been showing up to demonstrate. On Labor Day 1992 2,000 people went to Hegins to protest the shoot with signs like "Hegins—The Shame of Pennsylvania" and "Thou Shalt Not Kill Anything." Local supporters of the event say the shoot is a town tradition that is more than a half century old and that it raises funds for a local park.

Wayne Pacelle, national director of The Fund for Animals, who was one of the protesters, said, "If you looked to find the cruelest event in the country, from Alaska to Florida, you'll land in Hegins on Labor Day. It's the most barbaric slaughter of animals in the country."[2]

Pennsylvania animal advocates and other concerned citizens are trying to get the state legislature to outlaw bird shoots in the state, but so far they have been unsuccessful.

Animal rights volunteers treat wounded pigeons at an emergency first-aid station in Hegins, Pennsylvania, on September 7, 1992. Every Labor Day, the town sponsors a shoot that kills more than 6,000 pigeons.

Trapping

In the United States more than 30 million beavers, raccoons, coyotes, wolves, bobcats, lynxes, opossums, muskrats, otters, rabbits, and other animals are killed in traps each year, making this country the world's biggest trapper nation. Although most trappers kill animals for their fur, only a tiny percentage (about 1%) of them are professional trappers. The rest trap in their spare time to earn extra money or for recreation. The average non-professional trapper makes only about $100 a year from his trapping.

The most commonly used trap is the steel-jaw leghold trap that has a spring and steel jaws that clamp shut on the animal's leg. As the trapped animal struggles to free itself, the jaws sink more deeply and painfully into its leg. Although most states have regulations about how often traps must be checked, these regulations are frequently ignored. A trapped animal may survive for days or even weeks only to die from shock, blood loss, starvation, dehydration, infection, predators, or cold weather. Sometimes, in order to escape, the animal will chew or twist off its trapped leg. Trapped mothers desperately try to escape to return to their young whom they know will starve without them.

Trappers try to kill the animal without damaging its fur. They may do this by clubbing the animal, hitting it against a tree, or suffocating it by standing on its neck. A

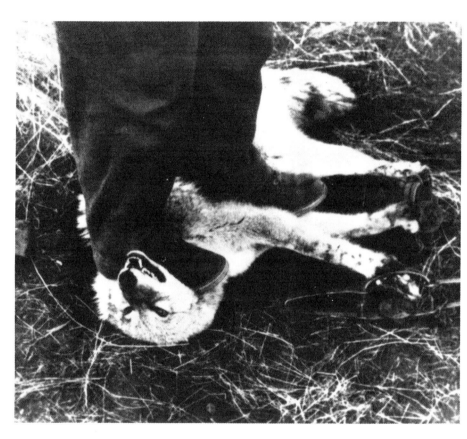

This trapper is standing on the neck of the coyote he caught in his leghold trap. Most trappers try to kill the animals they catch in ways that will not damage their fur.

reporter who accompanied a trapper described what happened when the trapper found a raccoon in his trap:

> With a carpenter's hammer that is standard equipment on his trap line, he aimed a blow at the raccoon's head. When the trapper opened the jaws of the trap, the raccoon, frothing blood, attempted to crawl away. With one quick motion the trapper grabbed the wounded animal by its hind legs, swung the body in a smooth arc and crunched its skull against a log. That ended the raccoon's struggles, his life traded for his fur. On that day, his fur was worth $12 for the trapper.[3]

Every year more than five million animals accidentally get caught in traps. They include dogs, cats, squirrels, hawks, owls, eagles, ducks, frogs, and sometimes even human children. Trappers call these accidents "trash" because they don't bring in any money. More than 65 countries have banned the steel-jaw leghold trap, as have nine American states. Still, the United States remains the largest user of the leghold trap and the biggest fur-producer in the world.

The Fur Controversy

Fur coats used to be symbols of beauty, fashion, glamour, success, and wealth, but that is changing as the public learns more about what goes into the making of fur coats. To make just one coat it takes 30 raccoons, 50 muskrats, 16 coyotes, 18 bobcats, 45 opossums, 15 beavers, 20 otters, 42 foxes, or 65 minks.

Today more furs come from fur farms (also called fur ranches) than from animals trapped in the wild. These fur farms range from small family businesses with as few as 50 animals to large businesses with many thousands of animals. In the United States there are approximately 750 chinchilla farms, 970 mink farms, and 3,000 fox farms.

The fur industry would like the public to think that ranch-raised animals don't suffer, but they do. Since fur farms want to keep their expenses to a minimum, the animals are kept in small wire cages, often in open sheds that provide little protection from the rain, wind, and cold. The animals only live a fraction of their natural lifespans before they are killed. Foxes are put to death when they are nine months old, minks when they are five months old. Breeding females are kept alive as long as they can produce offspring. When they can no longer bear young, they too are killed for their fur. Animals on fur farms are killed by suffocation, poison, gassing, or electrocution; in the case of small animals like minks and chinchillas, the method is breaking their necks. The most humane method would be a lethal injection, but that costs too much.

Anti-fur protests have brought the issue to the attention of the public. Every year on "Fur-Free Friday"—the day after Thanksgiving, which is the biggest shopping day of the year—demonstrations against fur are held across the country. Some American furriers have gone out of business, while others have been forced to sell their merchandise at reduced prices. In Europe the anti-fur campaign has caused fur sales to decline dramatically.

The fur industry and those who wear fur believe people have the right to raise and kill animals for the sake of style and comfort. Furriers are fighting back against the anti-fur campaign with increased advertising and new lines of coats with fur trim only or with a fur lining inside the coat where people won't see it.

Rodeos and Circuses

Rodeos began as contests of skill between cowboys, but today they have become money-making "wild west" shows. The Professional Rodeo Cowboys Association reports that rodeos bring in for their sponsors and host cities between 10 and 13 million dollars a year. "Ordinarily, I'd never do anything to hurt a calf," said one manager, "but when you're doing it for money, it's a different story."

In the calf-roping event it is common for calves to suffer torn ligaments, pulled muscles, and broken bones. In bull and wild horse riding events the normally gentle bulls and horses are provoked with electric prods, sharp sticks, painful ointments, and bucking straps designed to force them into "bronco" behavior. After rodeo animals are injured or their health deteriorates, they are sent to slaughter.

The veterinarian Charles Haber described the condition of the animals he saw brought to the slaughterhouse: "I have seen cattle so extensively bruised that the only areas in which the skin was attached was the head, neck, legs, and belly. I have seen animals with six to eight ribs broken from the spine and at times puncturing the lungs. I have seen as much as two or three gallons of free blood accumulated under the attached skin."[4]

While a circus can be a source of entertainment, life isn't much fun for circus animals. When the animals aren't performing, they are kept in small cages or transport vehicles. They are declawed, defanged, and often tranquilized so they won't pose a threat to their trainers. Trainers have been known to use whips, chains, muzzles, collars, and electric prods to get animals to do their tricks. Standing on one foot and jumping through a flaming hoop are two of the tricks circus animals are forced to perform.

When their performing days are over, circus animals are either put to death or sold to a travelling zoo, hunting ranch, or research lab. Two American cities—Takoma Park, Maryland, and Hollywood, Florida—have passed laws that restrict or ban the use of animals in circuses. Toronto, the second-largest city in Canada, recently outlawed shows with performing animals. England, Switzerland, Sweden, and Finland have similar laws.

Zoos

Although some claim zoos are more entertainment than education, zoos can provide a positive learning experience to people who want to observe and study animals. When

A worker lines up a row of circus elephants for transportation to another city. In his right hand he is holding an electric prod.

zoos were first established in the United States, the animals were trapped in the wild and kept in small cages.

Often an entire family was killed to capture a young animal. Today most zoo animals are bred in captivity although new animals have to be captured in the wild.

Large modern zoos and wildlife parks allow their animals to live in a more natural environment. Those who visit must remain behind barriers or on designated paths. However, in small city zoos and roadside zoos animals are kept in cages, some of them not much larger than the animals.

Supporters of zoos point out that animals in the wild are losing their habitats at an alarming rate. The only hope for saving threatened species, they say, is to preserve them in captivity. However, critics maintain that zoos are mostly out to make money and that even well-maintained zoos reinforce the idea that it is permissible to capture animals and put them on display to satisfy our curiosity. They say wild animals should be preserved and protected in their natural habitats.[5]

7
RESCUE AND REFUGE

Several large animal rights organizations send out their own researchers to investigate laboratories, supply houses, stockyards, schools, or any other institutions where they think animal abuse might be taking place. Although these investigations sometimes lead to criminal prosecutions, more often it is public exposure that brings the mistreatment to an end.

For example, in the fall of 1991 The Fund for Animals, a national animal rights organization, accused a high school in Basin, Wyoming, of animal abuse after it found out the school's rifle class went pigeon shooting on a teacher's farm. The group wrote the school—and newspapers in Wyoming and Montana as well—threatening to take legal action. As a result of their action, the practice was stopped.[1]

Some people and groups have established their own places of refuge for rescued animals. Although these sanctuaries can care for only a relatively small number of animals, they do provide safety to animals who need protection.

Noah's Ark (Georgia)

Jama Hedgecoth is founder and director of Noah's Ark, a sanctuary in Locust Grove, Georgia, which serves as a haven for injured and orphaned animals. She worked with animals as a dog breeder, animal trainer, and pet-pig rancher for 30 years before she began the unique animal rehabilitation center she now operates on her family farm about an hour south of Atlanta.

Hedgecoth and her family (parents, husband, and four children), assisted by ten full-time and four part-time volunteers, take care of injured wildlife and release the animals back into the wild when they are healthy again. Orphaned baby birds are given nightly feedings so they can be released when they are ready. If an animal does not recover well enough to search for food or defend itself, the animal then becomes a permanent resident. The approximately 700 animals at Noah's Ark include dogs, cats, horses, goats, wolves, foxes, cougars, deer, monkeys, birds, owls, geese, turkeys, eagles, peacocks, parrots, rabbits, possums, raccoons, and a llama.

These are two fawns at Noah's Ark Rehabilitation Center in Georgia. The fawn on the left was found by the side of an interstate highway next to her mother who was killed by a truck.

Noah's Ark also has a program that brings physically, mentally, and emotionally handicapped people to the farm to be with the animals. Some of the animals are also taken to nursing homes, children's homes, and prisons. Hedgecoth says the animals bring out the best in people. An animal doesn't care what a person looks like, she says, or if somebody is handicapped or retarded. "My enjoyment is bringing animals and people together, especially people who are hurting. My favorite is when the handicapped children visit. It makes me realize how fortunate I am when I see how excited they get with the animals."

Jama Hedgecoth hopes to build a center on her land that will make it easier to bring young and old together with animals. The center would be both a nursing home for the elderly and a home for abused, orphaned, and neglected children.[2]

Black Beauty Ranch (Texas)

Black Beauty Ranch is a 605-acre refuge for animals in northeast Texas owned and operated by The Fund for Animals. In 1979 when Cleveland Amory, the writer who heads the Fund, learned the National Park Service was going to destroy a herd of wild burros who lived in the Grand Canyon, he convinced the park officials to let him rescue the burros. With the help of helicopters, cowboys, and other volunteers he airlifted 577 burros out of the Grand Canyon.

Two burros scratch each other at Black Beauty Ranch in Texas. Friendly (rear), one of the ranch's longest residents, was rescued from the Grand Canyon in 1979. The other burro, Granny, pulled a farmer's plow for many years.

Besides some of the original burros still at Black Beauty Ranch, there are goats, sheep, pigs, deer, buffalo, foxes, raccoons, veal calves, geese, llamas, and horses. Nim the chimpanzee was famous before he arrived. For a university study Nim learned to communicate in sign language, using 125 hand signs. He was the subject of a doctoral dissertation and two books, and was on television. After the study was over however, the scientists had no more use for Nim. When The Fund for Animals found out he was going to be shipped off to a research laboratory at the State University of New York to test a hepatitis vaccine, the Fund convinced university officials to release him into their custody. That was ten years ago. Today Nim has a companion, Sally, a chimpanzee who was rescued from a circus act where she had been trained to ride a bicycle.

Conga, the elephant, is another star. After animal traders stole her from her mother in Africa, they sent her to the United States where she ended up in a roadside zoo in Florida. After enduring years of electric shocks to make her perform her tricks, she was replaced by a younger elephant. Conga used to be the only elephant at Black Beauty Ranch, but no more. A friend of the Fund rescued a sick and badly injured baby female elephant from a road show. The friend nursed the baby elephant back to health and named it Nora. She contacted Black Beauty Ranch, and the ranch agreed to give Nora a home.

The manager of the Black Beauty Ranch built a paddock next to Conga's compound in anticipation of Nora's arrival. He didn't want to put Conga and Nora together right away. He wanted to give Nora time to get used to Conga. "Their 'trial separation' lasted about 20 minutes," he said, "and then I couldn't stand it any longer. I let Conga in, and she brought Nora right back with her to the big compound. They've been together ever since."[3]

Farm Sanctuary (New York State)

Farm Sanctuary is a refuge for abused farm animals in upstate New York. In 1986 Gene and Lorri Bauston rescued Hilda, a woolly grey sheep, at a stockyard they were investigating. They discovered Hilda on a pile of dead animals. When they saw she was still alive, they took her home and nursed her back to health. That was how Farm Sanctuary began.

The Baustons started out with a donated house in Delaware, then moved to a borrowed farm in Pennsylvania. By the fall of 1990 they had raised enough money to buy a 175-acre abandoned farm outside Watkins Glen in upstate New York.

Today Farm Sanctuary is home to more than 400 animals rescued from stockyards where they were injured and left for dead and from farms where investigations uncovered mistreatment. The century-old white farmhouse that houses staff members and interns serves as Farm Sanctuary headquarters. Nine newly built barns house the cattle, ducks, geese, pigs, goats, sheep, turkeys, chickens, and rabbits. Farm Sanctuary has accepted animals from as far away as California and Minnesota and has already placed more than 350 animals in carefully screened adoptive homes.

Farm Sanctuary investigates conditions in stockyards and auction houses. Their investigators photograph and videotape mistreatment and use the evidence to try to rally public support for better treatment of farm animals. Farm Sanctuary has launched a national campaign against the mistreatment of downers in American stockyards. It is urging Congress to pass "The Downed Animal Protection Act" that would provide comprehensive protection for sick and injured farm animals.

Farm Sanctuary has also organized demonstrations on behalf of abused farm animals at the Lancaster Stockyards in Pennsylvania and the South Saint Paul Livestock Market in Minnesota. Although a number of stockyards have agreed not to accept downers, Farm Sanctuary investigations have shown that this mistreatment of sick and injured farm animals continues.[4]

Other Animal Sanctuaries

The largest animal rights group in the country—People for the Ethical Treatment of Animals (PETA)—has its own sanctuary in Silver Spring, Maryland, just north of Washington, D.C. Situated on eight acres of land donated to PETA in 1988, the Aspin Hill Memorial Park and Animal

Sanctuary is home to numerous sheep, rabbits, turkeys, chickens, dogs, cats, goats, and ducks as well as wild squirrels, chipmunks, opossums, bats, and birds.

Aspin Hill—and most of the other sanctuaries discussed in this chapter—welcome visitors. Children and adults can visit for a day or more. If you wish to visit an animal sanctuary, you should write or call ahead of time (addresses are in the chapter notes in back).

Primarily Primates, a nine-acre sanctuary north of San Antonio, Texas, provides shelter, rehabilitation, and lifetime care to over 300 monkeys, apes, chimpanzees, and other primates. Most of the primates suffered injury, abuse, neglect, and improper care in roadside zoos, animal acts, or research labs and had not lived with other primates since they were infants. Primarily Primates nurses them back to physical and emotional health and tries to help them adjust to a more natural life with their own kind.

Caroline Gilbert runs a sanctuary exclusively for rabbits on her 30-acre farm in South Carolina. Rabbit Sanctuary is home to more than 200 rabbits who are fugitives from local shelters, commercial breeders, and research labs. Rabbits from the surrounding woods have also found refuge on her property.

Pat Derby is a former circus trainer who now heads the Performing Animal Welfare Society (PAWS), which fights for animals in movies, TV, theme parks, rodeos, circuses, and zoos. PAWS has its own 20-acre sanctuary in Galt, California, that has given refuge to bears, wolves, monkeys, a baboon, and an elephant rescued from roadside zoos, animal shows, and movie sets.

Shirley McGreal, who heads the International Primate Protection League (IPPL), has a colony of gibbon families on her property in Summerville, South Carolina. In 1992 the United Nations honored her for her outstanding work on behalf of gorillas, chimpanzees, orangutans, and other endangered victims of the illegal international primate trade. The primate trade is especially cruel because it involves poachers shooting mother primates so they can steal their babies and sell them. People who want young primates as research subjects or pets will pay as much as $30,000 for them. [5]

"The Way of a Whole Human Being"

The term animal rights covers a wide range of groups and activities. Some animal advocates are primarily interested in animal shelters, the pet overpopulation problem, and anti-cruelty legislation. Others concentrate on wildlife and threatened species. Still others seek to improve the way farm and lab animals are treated.

The more radical members of the animal rights movement seek to abolish all forms of animal exploitation. These abolitionists believe that animals have an absolute moral right to lead their lives free of human interference. To achieve their goals, some animal advocates are willing to engage in direct action and civil disobedience.

For the animal rights movement to have a lasting impact it will need to win broad public support and translate its rhetoric into legislation and law enforcement. Since the idea of animal rights is still very new, the controversy will no doubt intensify in the years ahead. As the debate about rights—human and animal—heats up, we would all do well to recall the words of President Abraham Lincoln (1809–1865), who felt strongly about the issue. "I am in favor of animal rights as well as human rights," he said. "That is the way of a whole human being."

Notes By Chapter

Chapter 1

1. Steven Eisenstadt, "A Young Girl's Crusade Produces Bill to Limit Frog Dissection in School," *The Providence Journal* (May 7, 1992), p. A-1.

2. *Politics,* Everyman's Library (London: J. M. Dent & Sons, 1959), p. 16.

3. Quoted in Peter Singer, *Animal Liberation,* rev. ed. (New York: Avon, 1990), p. 7.

4. Laurence Pringle, *The Animal Rights Controversy* (San Diego, Calif.: Harcourt Brace Jovanovich, 1989), pp. 4–9.

Chapter 2

1. Bernice Kanner, "A Dog's Life—Love and Death at the ASPCA," *New York* (April 27, 1992), pp. 48–53.

2. States that do not permit pound seizure are Connecticut, Delaware, Hawaii, Maine, Maryland, Massachusetts, New Hampshire, New Jersey, New York, Pennsylvania, Rhode Island, South Carolina, Vermont, and West Virginia.

Chapter 3

1. Adrian R. Morrison, "What's Wrong With 'Animal Rights' " *American School Board Journal* (January 1992), pp. 20–23.

2. Louis Jacobson, "Animal-Rights Battle Spills into Schools as Both Sides Target Next Generation," *Wall Street Journal* (September 2, 1992), p. B1.

3. Student Action Corps for Animals is a nonprofit educational organization that helps students know and defend their rights. The group's newsletter, *SACA NEWS,* serves as a forum for the exchange of ideas among students. For more information contact: Student Action Corps for Animals, P.O. Box 15588, Washington, D.C. 20003-0588; (202) 543-8983.

4. About 60 percent of the calls to the hotline have been from high schools students, 30 percent from college students, and 10 percent from elementary school students. For more information contact: Animal Legal Defense Fund, 1363 Lincoln Avenue, Suite 7, San Rafael, CA 94901; (415) 459-0885.

5. Kathryn Winiarski, "Dissection Hot Line Cuts It," *The New York Times* (January 6, 1991), p. 10, EDUC.

6. American Anti-Vivisection Society press release, July 10, 1992.

7. For a copy of the NABT position statement contact: National Association of Biology Teachers, 11250 Roger Bacon Drive 19, Reston, VA 22090; (703) 471-1134.

8. Gary L. Francione and Anna E. Charlton, *Vivisection and Dissection in the Classroom: A Guide to Conscientious Objection* (Jenkintown, Penn.: American Anti-Vivisection Society, 1992), p. vii.

9. For information about nonanimal alternatives in veterinary education, write to: Association of Veterinarians for Animal Rights (AVAR), P.O. Box 6269, Vacaville, CA 95696-6269.

Chapter 4

1. Charles S. Nicoll and Sharon M. Russell, "Mozart, Alexander the Great, and the Animal Rights/Liberation Philosophy," *Federation of American Societies for Experimental Biology Journal* (November 1991), p. 2888. Opponents of animal research disagree with their claim. According to the American Anti-Vivisection Society (801 Old York Road, Jenkintown, PA 19046), two-thirds of the Nobel prizes in medicine and physiology have been awarded to researchers who primarily or entirely used methods that did *not* use animals.

2. *The Compassionate Quest* (pamphlet). For more information contact: North Carolina Association for Biomedical Research, P.O. Box 25459, Raleigh, NC 27611-5459.

3. For more information write to: Medical Research Modernization Committee, P.O. Box 6036, Grand Central Station, New York, NY 10163-6018; Physicians Committee for Responsible Medicine, P.O. Box 6322, Washington,

D.C. 20015; American Medical Association, 515 North State Street, Chicago, IL 60610.

4. Richard Weiskopf, M.D., "Animal Research Is Wasteful," *Syracuse Post-Standard* (January 14, 1992), p. A9.

5. Massachusetts Society for Medical Research, 1991 Annual Report. For more information contact: MSMR, 1440 Main Street, Waltham, MA 02154-1646; (617) 891-4544. Further information supportive of the use of animals in research may be obtained by contacting the following organizations:

National Association for Biomedical Research, 818 Connecticut Avenue, NW, Suite 303, Washington, DC 20006; (202) 857-0540.

Incurably Ill for Animal Research, P.O. Box 56093, Tucson, AZ 85703; (602) 682-5749.

Office of Animal Research Issues, Alcohol, Drug Abuse and Mental Health Administration, Room 12C-15, 5600 Fishers Lane, Rockville, MD 20857; (301) 443-0009.

6. Incurably Ill for Animal Research Report (Winter, 1991), p. 1.

7. For a list of companies that do not test on animals write to:

The Humane Society of the United States, 2100 L Street, NW, Washington, D.C. 20037.

Beauty Without Cruelty, 175 W. 12th Street, New York, NY 10011-8275.

People for the Ethical Treatment of Animals, P.O. Box 42516, Washington, D.C. 20015.

8. Quoted in Peter Singer (ed.), *In Defense of Animals* (New York: Harper & Row, 1986), p. 136.

9. Massachusetts Society for Medical Research News (January/February, 1992), p. 3.

10. Department of Health and Human Services, *Animal Research: The Search for Life Saving Answers*, p. 7.

Chapter 5

1. Jim Mason and Peter Singer, *Animal Factories,* rev. ed. (New York: Harmony Books, 1990), p. 2.

2. Jim Mason, "Food for Thought," *The AV Magazine* (October 1992), p. 14.

3. Quoted in Laurence Pringle, *The Animal Rights Controversy* (San Diego, Calif.: Harcourt Brace Jovanovich, 1989), p. 38.

4. Marian Burros, "Eating Well," *The New York Times* (July 8, 1992), p. C3.

5. For information about *HOW ON EARTH!*—a vegetarian newsletter by and for teens—contact Sally Clinton, Director, Vegetarian Education Network, P.O. Box 3347, Chester, PA 19380; (215) 696-VNET.

Chapter 6

1. Jon Wynne-Tyson (ed.), *The Extended Circle: A Commonplace Book of Animal Rights* (New York: Paragon House, 1989), p. 91.

2. Michael Stetz and Bill Savitsky, "114 Arrested at Pigeon Shoot," *Harrisburg Patriot-News* (September 8, 1992), p. 1.

3. Friends of Animals, "Take A Stand On Fur," pp. 1-2. For more information contact: Friends of Animals, P.O. Box 1244, Norwalk, CT 06856; (203) 866-5223.

4. International Society for Animal Rights, "Focus on Rodeos" Fact Sheet.

5. Zoe Weil, *Animals in Society: Facts and Perspectives on Our Treatment of Animals* (Jenkintown, Penn.: Animalearn, 1991), pp. 36–7.

Chapter 7

1. *American School Board Journal* (January 1992), p. 23.

2. For more information contact: Noah's Ark, 1425 Locust Grove Road, Locust Grove, GA 30248; (404) 957-0888.

3. For more information contact: Black Beauty Ranch, P.O. Box 367, Murchison, TX 75778; (903) 469-3811. Black Beauty Ranch has burros and horses available for adoption.

4. For more information contact: Farm Sanctuary, P.O. Box 150, Watkins Glen, NY 14891; (607) 583-2225.

5. For more information about these organizations contact:

Aspin Hill Memorial Park and Animal Sanctuary, 13630 Georgia Avenue, Silver Spring, MD 20906; (301) 871-6700.

Primarily Primates, P.O. Box 15306, San Antonio, TX 78212-8506; (512) 755-4616.

Rabbit Sanctuary, P.O. Box 365, Simpsonville, SC 29681; (803) 963-4389.

Performing Animals Welfare Society (PAWS), P.O. Box 849, Galt, CA 95632; (916) 393-3340 [Office]; (209) 745-2606 [Shelter].

International Primate Protection League, P.O. Box 766, Summerville, SC 29484; (803) 871-2280.

FURTHER READING

Achor, Amy Blount. *Animal Rights: A Beginner's Guide.* Yellow Springs, Ohio: WriteWare, 1992.

Animal Welfare Institute. *Animals and Their Legal Rights: A Survey of American Laws from 1641 to 1990.* Washington, D.C.: Animal Welfare Institute, 1990.

Asimov, Isaac. *Asimov's Biographical Encyclopedia of Science and Technology* (rev. ed.). New York: Doubleday, 1982.

Committee on Use of Laboratory Animals in Biomedical and Behavioral Research, National Research Council and Institute of Medicine. *Use of Laboratory Animals in Biomedical and Behavioral Research.* Washington, D.C.: National Academy Press, 1988.

Department of Health and Human Services. *Animal Research: The Search for Life-Saving Answers.* Washington, D.C.: Alcohol, Drug Abuse, and Mental Health Administration, 1991.

Dunayer, Eric. *Alternatives to the Harmful Use of Nonhuman Animals.* Vacaville, Calif.: Association of Veterinarians for Animal Rights, 1990.

Early Times. *Animal Kind.* London: Puffin Books, 1991.

Foundation for Biomedical Research. *The Use of Animals in Biomedical Research and Testing.* Washington, D.C.: Foundation for Biomedical Research, 1988.

Francione, Gary L., and Anna E. Charlton. *Vivisection and Dissection in the Classroom: A Guide to Conscientious Objection.* Jenkintown, Penn.: American Anti-Vivisection Society, 1992.

Jasper, James M., and Dorothy Nelkin. *The Animal Rights Crusade: The Growth of a Moral Protest.* New York: The Free Press, 1992.

Klaper, M.D., Michael. *Vegan Nutrition: Pure and Simple.* Paia, Maui, Hawaii: Gentle World, 1987.

Kowalski, Gary. *The Souls of Animals.* Walpole, N.H.: Stillpoint Publishing, 1991.

Mason, Jim, and Peter Singer. *Animal Factories* (rev. ed.). New York: Harmony Books, 1990.

Moran, Victoria. *Compassion: The Ultimate Ethic* (3rd ed.). Malaga, N.J.: American Vegan Society, 1991.

National Academy of Sciences, Institute of Medicine. *Science, Medicine, and Animals.* Washington, D.C.: National Academy Press, 1991.

Newkirk, Ingrid. *Free the Animals!: The Untold Story of the U.S. Animal Liberation Front and Its Founder, "Valerie".* Chicago: Noble Press, 1992.

Newkirk, Ingrid. *Kids Can Save the Animals!: 101 Easy Things To Do.* New York: Warner, 1991.

North Carolina Association for Biomedical Research. *The Compassionate Quest.* (pamphlet) Raleigh, N. C.: North Carolina Association for Biomedical Research.

Pringle, Laurence. *The Animal Rights Controversy.* San Diego, Calif.: Harcourt Brace Jovanovich, 1989.

Regan, Tom. *The Case for Animal Rights.* Berkeley: University of California Press, 1983.

Regan, Tom. *The Struggle for Animal Rights.* Clarks Summit, Penn.: International Society for Animal Rights, 1987.

Robbins, John. *Diet for a New America.* Walpole, N.H.: Stillpoint Publishing, 1987.

Singer, Peter. *Animal Liberation* (rev. ed.). New York: Avon, 1990.

Singer, Peter (ed.). *In Defense of Animals.* New York: Harper & Row, 1986.

Spiegel, Marjorie. *The Dreaded Comparison: Human and Animal Slavery.* New York: Mirror Books, 1989.

U.S. Congress, Office of Technology Assessment. *Alternatives to Animal Use in Research, Testing, and Education.* Washington, D.C.: U.S. Government Printing Office, 1986.

Weil, Zoe. *Animals in Society: Facts and Perspectives on Our Treatment of Animals.* Jenkintown, Penn.: Animalearn, 1991.

Wynne-Tyson, Jon (ed.). *The Extended Circle: A Commonplace Book of Animal Rights.* New York: Paragon House, 1989.

INDEX

A alternatives to dissection, 5–7, 34–37
American Heart Association, 71
American Museum of Natural History, 11–13
American Society for the Prevention of Cruelty to Animals (ASPCA), 8–10, 21
Amory, Cleveland, 92
animal labs, 38–39
Animal Legal Defense Fund, 36, 57
Animal Liberation, 10–11, 60
animal research, 24–25, 41–57
animal rights movement, 10–14, 98–99
Animal Welfare Act, 55–57
anti-fur protests, 84–85
anti-vivisection societies, 10
Aristotle, 8
Barger, Dr. A. Clifford, 48
Bauston, Gene and Lorri, 95
Bentham, Jeremy, 8
Bergh, Henry, 8–10

Bible, 7–8
Binkowski, Gloria, 39
birds, 5, 28, 56–57, 90, 97
biology, 28–37
biomedical research, 24–25, 41–48, 55–57
bird shoots, 78–80
Black Beauty Ranch, 92–95
broiler chickens, 61–62
bullfights, 73–74
burros, 92–94

C calves, 60, 64–66
cats, 11–13, 17–20, 24–25, 31, 40–41, 47, 56, 83, 90, 97
cattle, 66–67, 95
chickens, 28, 60–63, 95, 97
chimpanzees, 41, 94, 97
circuses, 86–87, 97
classroom, animals in, 28
Congress, 13, 55, 96
cows, 41, 60, 62–64, 75
cruelty-free, 52

D dairy products, 62–64, 71
Derby, Pat, 97
DeBakey, Dr. Michael, 57
deer, 74, 90, 94
Descartes, René, 8
dissection, 28–37
dissection hotline, 36

dogs, 5,8,17–20, 23–25, 27, 38–40, 42, 46–49, 56, 75, 83, 97
downers, 67–68, 96
Draize Eye Irritancy Test, 49–51
Dunayer, Eric, 34, 39

E education, animals in, 27–40
eggs, 60, 62–63
elephants, 94–95, 98
euthanasia, 20–22

F factory-farming, 60–72
farm animals, 59–72, 95–96, 98
Farm Sanctuary, 61, 95–96
food animals, 59–72
Food Animals Concern Trust, 61
frogs, 28–37, 83
Fund for Animals, 79, 89
fur, 81–85
"Fur-Free Friday", 84

G Gallup Youth Survey, 13
Gandhi, Mohandas K., 74
Gilbert, Caroline, 97
Graham, Jenifer, 28–31, 36
Graham, Pat, 30, 36
guinea pigs, 5, 28, 49, 56

H Hedgecoth, Jama, 90–92

hormones, 64
horses, 10, 75, 90, 94
Humane Society of the United States, 30, 56–57
hunt sabotages, 75–77
hunting, 74–80, 89
hunting ranches, 77–78

K Koop, Dr. C. Everett, 51

L laboratory animals, 24–25, 41–57, 97–98
layer hens, 62–63
LD (Lethal Dose) 50 Test, 48–50
Lincoln, Abraham, 99
livestock, 66–70

M McGreal, Shirley, 98
medical schools, 27, 38–39
mice, 31, 41, 49, 50, 56–57
monkeys, 37, 45, 52–56, 90, 97
Morrison, Dr. Adrian, 33

N National Association of Biology Teachers, 37
National Science Teachers Association, 37
neutering, 18–20, 40
Noah's Ark Rehabilitation Center, 90–92
non-animal alternatives, 38–40, 51

O Olympics, 73

P Pacelle, Wayne, 79
Pacheco, Alex, 52–55
People for the Ethical Treatment of Animals (PETA), 96
Performing Animal Welfare Society (PAWS), 97
pet overpopulation problem, 15–22
pet stores, 23–24
pigeon shooting, 78–80, 89
pigs, 41, 60, 66–67, 69, 94, 95
pithing of frogs, 31–33
poultry, 61–62
pound seizure, 24–25
Primarily Primates, 97
primates, 37, 41, 45, 52–56, 97–98
Proctor & Gamble, 51
product testing, 24, 42, 48–52
puppy mills, 23–24

R Rabbit Sanctuary, 97
rabbits, 49–51, 81, 90, 96, 97
rain forests, 70
rats, 31, 41, 49, 56–57
rodeos, 85–86, 97
Rosen, Georgi, 5–7

S sanctuaries, 90–98
Silver Spring monkeys, 52–56
sheep, 41, 94, 95, 97
shelters, 15–17, 20–22, 24–25, 40, 97
Singer, Peter, 10–11, 60
sows, 66
spaying, 18–20, 40
speciesism, 11
steel-jaw leghold traps, 81–83
stockyards, 67, 96

T Taub, Dr. Edward, 52–55
trapping, 81–83

U United Nations, 98
United States Department of Agriculture (USDA), 23, 56–57, 64

V veal calves, 64–67, 94
vegans, 71–72
vegetarians, 71–72
Veterinarians for Animal Rights, 34
veterinary schools, 27, 39–40
vivisection, 10

W Weiskopf, Dr. Richard, 44
worms, 31, 36

Z zoos, 86–88, 97–98